BETTER
than
BEACH
MONEY

Published by Motivational Press, Inc.
1777 Aurora Road
Melbourne, Florida, 32935
www.MotivationalPress.com

Manufactured in the United States of America.

ISBN: 978-1-62865-450-9

BETTER
than
BEACH MONEY

JORDAN ADLER

MOtivational PRESS®
LEADERS IN GLOBAL PUBLISHING

This book is for the
Dreamer who is Stuck.

Contents

BETTER

than

BEACH MONEY

Credits

All of the stories in this book are true and were inspired by the following special people in my life (and a bird). My life is my life because of you.

My Father, Herbert Adler
My Mother, Rhoda Adler
Al Thomas, Mentor
Curtis Broome, Consultant
The Pelican, Bird
Dianna Haun, Former Boss
Jack Birnbuam, Former Bosses Boss
Daniel Boone, Former Boss
Dan McManus, Hang Gliding Instructor
Jan Johnson, Sage
Almas and Katia Meirmanov, Circus Performer and American Ninja Warrior
Andrel Robl, Professional Poker Player
My Sister, Audrey Adler
My Sister, Donna Adler
Rose Kingscote, Virgin Galactic
Richard Branson, You know who he is
Caroline Ferguson, Travel Agent to Space
Buddy Mondlock, Musician, Story Teller and Writer
Art Garfunkel, of Simon and Garfunkel
Gwen Field, Movie Producet
Gary Pearl, Executive Producer, Jane the Virgin
Robbie Williams, Biggest Pop-Star in Europe

Alex the Tailor, Makes clothing
Rob Vaca, Founder, Equity Estates
David Martin, Philanthropist
Celine Truong, Philanthropist
Eric and Marina Worre, Network Marketing Pro
Brian and Bianco Lorenz, Owners, 702 Helicopters
Travis Van Den Broeke, Helicopter Certified Flight Instructor
Kody Bateman, CEO and Founder SendOutCards
John Dawson, Owner, Scottsdale Plaza Resort
Alistair Humphries, Adventurer, Author and Speaker
CaSandra Smith, Networker
Donna Johnson, Top Network Marketer
Thomas Tidland, Top Network Marketer

Preface

Children spot each other. Dogs spot each other. And entrepreneurs spot each other. Have you ever noticed that when walking in a crowd, a child will notice another child and stare? The same goes for dogs. We as entrepreneurs do the same thing. We are different. We are usually the odd ones that others talk about when we have our backs turned. They think we are crazy. And in some ways we are. We see life through a different set of lenses and that makes us unique. Our viewpoint allows us to see things that others never get to see. And the experience of knowing we are different makes us attracted to ideas, opportunities and to each other. We want to share our unique point of view with others. And sharing our experiences with others who see things the way we do is . . . Better than Beach Money.

The most significant thing that I have learned is there is always another way to look at things. And by opening up my mind to the idea that my perspective may be holding me back and that a fresh perspective could be exactly what I need to grow, I have been able to create a whole new world of opportunity for myself and for others.

Being stuck or producing mediocre results is a temporary condition, as long as we continue to pursue new perspectives. Every breakthrough is born out of a shift in viewpoint that transforms how a set of circumstances is perceived. Sometimes a minor shift can create a big breakthrough. Whenever I'm stuck or looking for a radical change in results, I pursue a change in my point of view.

This book is *Better than Beach Money*. Beach Money pays you over and over again for working one time. No one can dispute that it's better to get paid multiple times for working once, instead of getting paid one time for working over and over.

I used to dream of a day I could retire on the beach and not have to wait until I'm old and broken down to do it. I knew that, based on my current job income, my government retirement check would be in the range of $1,000-$2,000 per month, and I would have to wait until I was 65 to receive it. There was the big question: Would it even be around when I reached retirement age? To be able to create a monthly passive income while I was still young enough to enjoy it sounded pretty good!

At age 34, I was still living in a 200 square foot enclosed garage paying $200 a month for rent. My twenty-two credit cards were maxed out to $36,000 and my jeep had been broken down in the street for two years. When I reflect on my situation back then, it's hard for me to believe this was actually me. I shopped for clothes at the thrift store. I gave plasma for cash. Bouncing checks was a monthly occurrence. And lack of money was daily challenge in my life. There was never enough of it.

If I had known how tough it was going to be to get out of the mess I was in, I don't know if I would have even started on the journey; but at the same time, knowing how good it would be on the other side of it all would have motivated me to do it all over again.

Today, I don't typically look at prices when I buy things. When ordering food in a restaurant, I order from the left side of the menu without looking at the prices on the right. I buy new clothes before my old ones wear out. And I shop from the stores that have the designs that I love versus shopping only where the prices are cheaper.

I didn't want to become someone who wears the same old clothes for years, well after they needed to be thrown away or used as an old rag. I drive cars that inspire me. I don't hesitate to pay a premium to buy tickets to an event to so I can sit up front. Concerts, shows and fights are way better when you are sitting in one of the front rows. I recently bought tickets from a broker to sit up front at the Billboard Music Awards for $1000 each. The show featured over 30 of the top musical artists of the year. I don't plan trips based on finances. I take trips when I want or need to go. I don't base my decision on whether I have the money to travel.

When my father was suffering from heart issues, I was able to fly to Chicago once a month for a full year to spend time with him in the hospital. My good friends, Eric and Marina Worre, recently invited me and some other friends to spend a couple of weeks on the beach in Bora Bora. The airfare and hotel came to $20,000 and our excursions for the week were about $10,000. Again, I didn't have to decide to go based on money. Money is rarely the issue anymore.

I was invited to attend a charity event in Minneapolis and sit at a table with some very successful entrepreneurs. The ticket for the table was $ 5000 and I purchased it without thinking about it. Life is better when you have Beach Money.

I had always dreamed of a day that money wouldn't be the main issue in my life. Most people say that money isn't the most important thing, yet most of their existence consists of worrying about it, talking about it and arguing about not having enough of it. The biggest fights most families have are about money. "You used the credit card for what? You know we can't even cover the monthly bills as it is!" "Why did you buy the $200 tires and wheels instead of the $100 ones? You know we can't afford that!" "Where have you been for the past four hours? Shopping again? What did you buy this time?"

The people that say, "Money isn't everything" are the same people that don't have much of it!

Let's face it: some days you don't want to go to work. In fact, some *months* you don't want to go to work! When you have Beach Money, you get to choose when you work and when you don't. You'll decide to take time off knowing that the money will continue to flow into your bank account. It feels really good to have the peace of mind that any money you spend this month will return next month.

I have a good friend that used to pull a $20 dollar bill out of his wallet and ask you to pull a $20 bill out of your wallet. He would then ask, "What's the difference between your $20 bill and my $20 bill?" After a blank stare and a long pause he would say, "The difference between my $20 bill and your $20 bill is that when I spend mine, it comes back!"

Beach Money is a great thing. It's the gift that keeps on giving. If you don't currently have Beach Money, I recommend that you work on it. You can learn how in my first book, *Beach Money*. If you're not living on beach money, then get Beach Money!

Beach Money is real.

Now, I know it's hard to believe but there is something *even better* than Beach Money. It lies in the stories and experiences that are created as a result of having a Beach Money lifestyle. You'll have a special "pass" to an aspect of life unavailable to most. And usually you don't see it until after you've achieved it. It's invisible and out of sight. What is *Better Than Beach Money*?

CONFUSED, FRUSTRATED AND EDUCATED

This is the fourth training event Shawn had attended this year. He always arrives early to be seated in the first or second row. He is a voracious note taker. He read that he will retain 30 percent more if he takes notes. He has been reading personal development books for at least ten years. He leans in as his favorite speaker takes the stage. He learns something new at every event.

Although he hasn't made much progress in his business so far, he's convinced that *this time* will be different. He's even tried a number of coaches over the years. He just completed an expensive nine-week, intensive group coaching program that promised to eliminate his fear of cold calling. It worked for a bit, but after about three weeks he was back to his old ways.

The fact is, Shawn was not much further along in his business than he was when he started. His business life has been a roller coaster of emotions. His personal life has been a roller coaster of emotions as well. He has gone through periods of focused effort, and has had dry spells that have lasted for weeks. Some months he is so motivated he can't sleep, and other months he is so depressed that nothing seems to go right. It's a miracle that he is still in the business. He loves the people and the idea of it, but he doesn't have much to show for his years of effort.

He follows the advice of his team leader, and many times makes sacrifices to attend the company events. He has purchased thousands of dollars in training programs. He wants this so bad he can taste it!

Sometimes Shawn questions himself and wonders if he is cut out to be an entrepreneur. He tries to stay positive, but the journey can be so frustrating. He has observed others breakout and create fantastic lifestyles, but he feels he might be missing something. It's just seems like an ongoing endless struggle.

Shawn is coachable and takes the advice of the authors, speakers and coaches who have gone before him, but most of it seems to make little difference. Some of his coaches have told him that the reason he isn't succeeding is because his "why" isn't big enough! So Shawn is working on getting a bigger why, something he's been trying to do for years. He knows that quitting isn't the answer. He knows that his current work situation isn't going to get him the lifestyle that he desires. It just all seems so baffling!

Shawn gets a pit in his stomach every time he has to go to work. His co-workers are getting on his nerves almost daily and his boss is incompetent. Besides that, he is completely uninspired by his chosen line of work. Many days he feels like an animal trapped in a cage. Life was not meant to be lived in this way. Shawn is continually haunted with the big question, "What am I doing wrong?"

Shawn's story is not the exception. Shawn's story is the norm. Most ambitious and hardworking wannabe entrepreneurs will repeat this pattern for years with little to no progress in their businesses. I was one of those people!

I had a library of audios and books and I did learn from them. However, what I learned made little difference in my results. In fact it made *no difference* in my results. I continued to plod along at less than a snail's pace for over ten years.

Nothing seemed to make a difference.

One time I was told that I wasn't enthusiastic enough. So I bought a couple of books and audios on enthusiasm and I tried to be more excited and positive every day. After a year of that, all my friends and family were saying they were sick of me being so excited and positive all the time. My mentors said that I needed to forget all the negative people and find others that were more like me! Three years later, I was no further along, except now I was a struggling positive wannabe entrepreneur!

One day everything changed. I figured out that what I had been looking for had little to do with hard work, enthusiasm or anything else I had learned. In fact, although my "why" kept getting stronger over the years, I became more and more frustrated. I was seeking to learn something in a seminar, in a book or in an audio. But none of it seemed to move the bar. Working harder didn't work. Going to more seminars didn't work. Expanding my "why" didn't work. Being more excited didn't work. Don't get me wrong; I believe in these things and encourage everyone to fully engage. But in terms of moving the bar—no difference.

So my intention for this book is for you to see something that you have never seen before. You may consider it a blindspot. By seeing it, you will be set free of the imaginary boundaries that are holding you back. You may gain some interesting or valuable insights from this book, but like most everything else we learn, these will most likely make little difference.

Knowing doesn't make a difference!

I hope to make the invisible, visible, in a way that will transcend anything you have learned in the past. And by seeing it come into focus, your life will never be the same.

HOW TO DO IT

Instructional training is important. I wouldn't want a surgeon operating on me if they hadn't been properly trained. I wouldn't want an airline pilot to be flying me around if they hadn't been schooled on how to safely fly an airplane. But to attend trainings year after year with little-to-no measurable results is irresponsible, if you are working to create a viable enterprise.

"If you keep looking in one place for the answer to your problem but the answer is hidden in another place, you will continue to search to no avail."

Everything in this book is true. The names are real. No characters have been changed or altered. The events really happened and have been represented as accurately as I, the author can remember them.

Your friend,

CHAPTER 1

The Entrance

I noticed the light, sweet scent of the fake smoke being pumped into the arena for effect. The footlights cut streaks of purple color through hazy puffs of theatrical clouds floating through the audience in the first five rows. I was standing at the bottom of the dimly lit stairs leading up to the back of the stage. Scuffed orange florescent tape was pealing from the black painted steps leading up to the stage. Beams of smoky light leaked through the cracks in the draped scaffolding, and the pounding music was my cue to be ready to run onto the stage as Curtis introduced me to the audience of over 5,000 enthusiastic entrepreneurs.

Due to the bright lights, I can only make out the faces of those in the first few rows, but I can always feel the electrically-charged energy of the crowd.

I was wired up with a Lavalier microphone that had been taped to the side of my face. As always, I had a tinge of nervousness waiting for my cue. One of the other speakers walked by and gave me a high five and jokingly said in his backstage voice, "Don't screw it up!"

Curtis's intro seemed to go a little longer than usual. As many times as I had done this, I still had to breathe into the experience, wondering how I got here. There was always a moment prior to entering the stage that felt surreal . . . like an out-of-body experience. It was like a drug that felt a little scary and exciting at the same time. And I was definitely addicted.

The voice from the stage echoed through the arena amplified by the sheer size of the place. Then I felt the vibration of a text coming from my phone from the inside pocket of my sports coat. I should have ignored it but instead I pulled it out seconds before walking on to the stage. The text was from my sister in Chicago: "Dad's going to die tonight."

THE RIGHT DECISION

My heart was in my throat. I got choked up as I processed the news. I was blinded for a moment by the intensity of never seeing my father again on this earth. I had to make a quick decision. My father had been ill with heart issues for almost a year, and we knew his days were numbered. It was Friday night and the event was in Las Vegas. I knew I couldn't get a flight back to Chicago that night, but would need to book something right away. I was also committed to being on that stage.

If I had informed the hosts that I couldn't do it, they would have walked on stage and made an announcement and everyone would have understood. I felt that in that moment I was being tested. I have taught thousands of business owners to make decisions based on commitment, not emotion.

However, seconds before entering the stage, my world was spinning out of control and taking on a crowd of 5000 people seemed more than I could handle. My legs began to get weak. I felt sick to my stomach and began to hyperventilate. Some close friends backstage saw that something was wrong and two of them came over to find out if I was okay. I told them what had happened and they wrapped their arms around me in an emotional moment.

Did I really believe what I had been teaching for so many years? Was I committed to being on that stage and delivering something of value to those who had taken valuable time, and chosen to be away from their families to be at this event?

I took a deep breath, looked up and told my friends that I needed to be on the stage. I had to live by what I had been teaching for so many years. My speech was only twenty minutes, and I immersed myself in the love radiating from the smiling faces coming from the first few rows of the audience. When it was over, I tearfully thanked my friends, then headed home to book my flight reservations. My father lived for two more weeks and I was thankful to be by his side for his final days on earth.

Everyone that fails quit on a bad day

Most people make their decisions based on how they are feeling in a given moment. This is one of the main reasons why so many business owners fail. If you choose to work only when things are good, at some point you will lose steam and give up. And the reason so many fail is because they quit on a bad day.

Everyone that fails quits on a bad day.

As humans, our emotions go up and down. It is normal to have good days and tough days. The key to success is to work your business on the good days *and* the tough days. Your greatest growth opportunities occur when you are experiencing challenges and choose to work through them instead of throwing in the towel. And you must do this over and over again to succeed in any business enterprise.

I have watched many talented dreamers fall flat on their faces in business over and over again because their pattern is to quit when things get difficult.

My "success" habit for my first ten years in business was to quit when I experienced any type of challenge. And quitting doesn't work as a success habit. Each time I got that pit in my stomach and started to question myself, I would set things aside and I was done. Then I would start over six to ten months later. This pattern is not the pattern of a successful leader or entrepreneur. I had lessons to learn, and each time I quit my business I was turning my back on the lessons needed to succeed and grow.

The pattern of a winner is to look for ways to make things work versus throwing in the towel. The pattern of a winner is to keep going when things get difficult.

I have adopted a philosophy that has served me over and over in my career. "Don't quit on a bad day!" Instead, I choose to work harder when things are tough. By doing this, I can transform a bad day into a good week. Or I can make a bad week a great month!

"Don't make your business decisions based on how you are feeling in any giving moment. Make your decisions based on what you are committed to. Never quit on a bad day."

CHAPTER 2

Born To Fly

The retreat was being held in Cancun, Mexico, at a secluded beachside resort. I was awakened by the howling wind forcing its way through the tiny crevices in the space between the sliding glass doors leading out to the balcony. Storms were in the forecast and the air felt unusually warm, thick and humid. I set the alarm for 5:30 a.m. so I could get a six o'clock workout, but the ominous weather woke me ten minutes before my alarm.

I kicked the sheets down to my feet and rolled over sideways, then I slung my legs over the side of the bed. I put my feet down on the carpet, pulled myself upright and stood for a moment as I found my balance and got my bearings straight. I am in a different hotel room almost weekly and sometimes it takes a minute to figure out what city I am in. It felt good to know I was waking up by the sea.

The air was heavy and salty. It was still dark outside, and I pulled back the curtains in my beachside hotel room. I gazed into the darkness, only to see the outline of water meeting the saturated clouds etched in the horizon. I cracked the sliding glass doors to feel the temperature of the warm ocean air. I then made my way to the bathroom, brushed my teeth in the dark and proceeded to throw on my gym clothes for a quick morning workout.

I stepped out onto my deck and took in a long deep breath. There were wooden steps leading from my hotel room deck down to the sand where the gym was on the beach. The thunderous waves crashed against shore in the wake of a huge storm that was building off in the distance.

I shifted my weight into an unnatural forward angle as I walked into the wind and down to the beach. I struggled to round the corner of the weathered wooden railing that led to the old beach gym. The windows had a film of saline, and the paint was peeling down to the gray and cracked raw wood on the windowsills.

I saw a slight movement out of the corner of my right eye. I shifted my glance and noticed the silhouette of a large pelican perched on a wooden post. I stared for a moment, then sat down on the worn, wooden steps that led up to gym doors. The pelican looked at me and I couldn't help but notice how strikingly perfect it was against the backdrop of the dark storm brewing in the distance. The sky was a shade between black and gray and the outline of the pelican was deep blue against the sky.

A moment later, the pelican slowly spread its large wings, and in an instant the wind picked it up into a hover. I squinted as I noticed a long tether around one of it's ankles! When the pelican reached the end of the tether, it was instantly yanked out of the air and tumbled down to the ground and into the sand.

Obviously shaken and unsure of what happened, the pelican stood up and gained its composure. It then opened its wings and with a big hop landed right back up on the post. About sixty seconds later, it spread its wings once again and hovered in the wind for a minute. Then it tried to fly away, only to be yanked back to the sand once more. I felt sorry for the bird and could feel it's frustration as it tried over and over again to fly. No amount of skill or natural flying ability could help the pelican as long as he was tethered to the post!

THE PELICAN'S ONLY HOPE

The Pelican's God-given birthright is to fly with the wind. Yet it was unable to fly.

Even the most skilled pelican coach could not teach this bird how to fly as long as he was bound by the tether. The confused pelican could try every flying trick in the pelican manual to no avail. As skilled a flyer as he was, until the pelican could figure out how to untether himself, he would not experience the true freedom of flight.

AN UNTRUTH

I did begin this book by telling you that all the stories are true. I did tell you the truth, with the exception of one tiny detail. There is only one thing in this story that is not true, and it is the littlest thing that makes the biggest difference. There never was a tether. The tether is a figment of my imagination. I imagined a tether attached to the pelican's leg and what it would do to the bird's ability to fly. Although the pelican had perfect flying abilities, its tether kept it from flying. The tether was nonexistent on the beach that morning.

Imaginary tethers are figments of our imagination. They are not real and they hold us back.

They keep us from flying and reaching our full potential. We were born to fly! Sometimes our inability to fly has nothing to do with our flying skills. Once we are able to see that we are tethered, and that the tethers are of our own creation, we are free to release them to go on to reach our full potential.

> Once we are able to see that we are tethered, and that the tethers are of our own creation, we are free to release them to go on to reach our full potential.

CHAPTER 3

Yellow Ropes

In my last job working as a corporate trainer for a major airline, I was introduced to an exercise that gave me great insight into what holds most people back from getting what they want. It's a simple idea that challenges conventional thinking. Most people believe that getting something requires learning the skills for success. Sometimes that's true. But more often than not, acquiring what we want is simply about removing imaginary boundaries—boundaries that do not exist.

Boundaries and limitations are self-imposed. Most of the time we already know how. It's not the *how* that is keeping us from getting what we want. It's the imaginary tethers that keep us bound to our past, putting our dreams just out of reach.

There is an exercise called Yellow Ropes. We enter a meeting room with six people and a group of observers. The observers must say nothing and are not allowed to coach in any way. One person stands in the center of the room and the other five are spaced along the walls at the perimeter of the room. The person in the center of the room is blindfolded.

Five yellow ropes are tied to the belt of the person in the middle. One rope is handed to each of the five participants standing along the perimeter of the room. A $20 bill is placed on the floor in a random location. The five participants holding the ends of the yellow ropes can see the bill, but the person blindfolded in the middle cannot.

I then give the instructions. The *only* rule: No verbal communication is allowed. The objective is for the person in the middle to get to the $20 bill and pick it up. We then start the exercise.

A couple of the participants holding the yellow ropes let theirs out, and one or two of the others pull theirs in, guiding the participant in the middle to be centered over the $20 bill. After a few minutes, the person in the middle bends over and picks up the money. Mission accomplished.

Now the exercise changes.

The five participants along the perimeter of the room are blindfolded and the person in the middle can see everything. The *only* rule: No verbal communication is allowed.

The $20 bill is again placed on the floor. The person in the middle can see it, but those along the perimeter against the wall cannot. The objective is for the person in the middle to get to the $ 20 bill and pick it up.

We start the exercise. The person in the middle attempts to send rope signals to the blindfolded participants holding the ropes. Not much happens. After a few minutes, frustration sets in. So I repeat the rules. The *only* rule: No verbal communication is allowed.

Again, the person in the middle attempts to send rope signals to those holding the ends of the ropes around the perimeter of the room to no avail. After a couple of minutes of frustration, I stop the exercise once again and repeat the only rule: "No verbal communication allowed."

SELF-IMPOSED LIMITATIONS

Usually after three rounds, the person in the middle figures out that I never said anything about the belt, the ropes or anything else. The only rule is the participants can't verbally communicate! The person in the middle finally figures out that he can take the belt off and walk right over to the $20 bill and pick it up.

Yellow ropes represent imaginary boundaries we create that keep us from getting what we want. More often than not, when our results are dismal, it has to do more with our self-imposed boundaries than our skill level. Skills are vitally important, but without recognizing our imaginary yellow ropes no amount of skill will make a difference. We can train incessantly and be well prepared. But if we are bound by our imaginary tethers, we will fail over and over again.

At any point, the person in the middle could have taken off the belt and walked right over the $20 bill. Valuable time was wasted. Lots of frustration could have been avoided had the person in the middle realized that the only rule was no verbal communication. Do you see there was no learning curve required? Picking up the twenty dollar bill had nothing to do with a learning curve or a skill. There was nothing to learn, only something to discover. Once you see the yellow ropes are not binding you to your past, you are free to walk right over and pick up the money.

WHAT ARE YOUR YELLOW ROPES?

What are you saying to yourself that is keeping you from walking right over and getting what you want? What beliefs about yourself or others are you holding on to that are keeping you from your dreams? Your dreams are in sight … and just out of reach. The yellow ropes usually represent stories you tell yourself that hold you back. Your dream life is just beyond your grasp because of the imaginary yellow ropes that are binding you to your past.

Most of the time we are fully capable.

The things holding us back are aren't real.

They don't exist.

They are things we are telling ourselves over and over again that keep us from walking over and getting what we want. We are holding on to what is easy and comfortable but also protects us from our imaginary fears. Taking bold risks, being more motivated, deploying massive action—none of it matters, if we continue to be tethered to our past.

Will you continue to be bound to your past, or are you really ready to release the imaginary yellow ropes holding you back? It's time to notice that *you* are the one holding on to the yellow ropes. You can't talk to people? Yellow rope! You're afraid to give a presentation? Yellow rope! You are too young or too old to succeed? Yellow rope!

Change the story and step into your new future. Let it go and go get what you want.

You are not smart enough? Yellow rope! You don't have the startup capital? Yellow rope! You are afraid you'll fail? Yellow rope! Do you see that all these yellow ropes are just made up stories we keep repeating to ourselves over and over again? Maybe it's time to take the belt off and abandon those yellow ropes forever!

You may wonder like most do how to release the yellow ropes? How do you release the imaginary, self-imposed boundaries keeping you inches away from your dreams? This is the most common question I'm asked on this topic. And your question is not relevant! The answer you seek will not be found in the realm of the how-to. Asking how to remove a yellow rope is like asking how to open a closed door. You already know how! You don't need to be taught. "How?" may not be the question that will lead you to the answer you seek. Again, there is no learning curve here. You have nothing to learn to break free.

There is no time required to break free. It can be done right now. Just drop the rope. Change the story and step in to your new future. Let it go and go get what you want.

When it comes to letting go of an imaginary boundary it's a simple decision to release it and move on; no need to take forever to try and figure things out. Remember you are holding on tight to something that doesn't even exist!

My friend and mentor Kody Bateman says, "The stories in your mind become the stories of your life. They aren't real when they begin!"

Your stories will either disempower you or they will serve you. Releasing old stories and creating new ones that allow you to step into your new future is one of the keys to personal growth.

CHAPTER 4

Finding Lift

As I leaned forward into the ocean of air where the forest meets the sky, I feel the weight of my body sink into the harness that supports me from a hook suspended in air. The rush of the wind intensifies as my feet gently leave the earth. I feel free. Silence is death when you are flying hang gliders. It means that you are no longer flying because the wind is no longer passing over the wing offering the lift that keeps it aloft. Flying on the wind is a spiritual experience. Bound by nothing. As I shift my weight to the left, my glider banks and the richness of the green mountain slowly comes into view over my left shoulder. The rippling sound of the Dacron wing flapping as it cuts through the air is a sign that all is well.

The wind is fresh and cool in my face.

But all is not well. The landing zone is five miles away. And assessing the mountainous terrain below tells me I need to gain some altitude before sinking down too low. The green forest foliage looks soft from above, but dropping a hang glider into dense mountain terrain is suicide. So I'm seeking lift. I have no motor to propel me. And I sink lower.

LEANING INTO LIFT

Dropping down any lower means big trouble. I shift my weight to the right away from the mountain hoping to catch some air. I can see the landing zone off in the distance. It's a tiny patch of beige desert about the size of my thumbnail beyond the golf course and just in front of the tiny airport. Clouds are building up in the distance.

Suddenly, without warning, I feel violent rush of warm air pass over me causing the rapid sensation of rising up. The rush of wind in my face intensifies to a light roar as the sensation of upward movement breaks the pattern of my downward flight path. I'm now gaining altitude and that's a good thing.

As the summer sun heats the desert floor, large invisible "bubbles" of air lift off and rise to the cooler temperature levels, forming those puffy cumulus clouds we see forming later in the afternoon in the western U.S. As a hang glider pilot, we seek out these massive columns of hot rising air to provide the "lift" we need to stay airborne for long periods of time.

Have you ever noticed a hawk circling above and staying aloft without ever flapping its wings? It is riding on the lift of the hot rising thermals. Much like the bubbles forming on the bottom of a glass of champagne, the warmer air is less dense, lighter and therefore rises up to meet the sky.

As a hang glider pilot, when you find lift, your objective is to shift your weight in the glider to "bank" into the center of it to maximize the opportunity rise up. When the air is extremely humid and unstable, we will notice formations of dark, heavy and thick cumulus clouds that are filled with electricity and moisture. These cloud formations can be very dangerous to a hang glider pilot, because they possess so much lift that a novice pilot can get caught up in the violent "cloud suck." The out-of-control pilot is lifted to altitudes of extreme cold and very thin air and ultimately freeze-dried and spit out by Mother Nature.

As a hang glider pilot, we learn that unstable air represents the opportunity for great lift. We seek it out to rise higher. Avoiding lift means a boring sleigh ride from the mountain top to the desert floor.

The greater the instability, the greater the lift.

INSTABILITY IS THE GIFT

As you read this, there may be areas in your life that feel challenging and unstable. The laws of nature dictate that, just like in a hang-glider, if you bank into the center of the instability, it will offer you the greatest opportunity for lift.

Our problems can feel like the end of the world. Life can be volatile, turbulent and unpredictable. The urge to resist our challenges is great because challenges can be uncomfortable. They can stop us or even hold us back. But by embracing our biggest obstacles and leaning into them, we can find the greatest opportunities for lift than at any other time of our lives. Lift is created by instability and volatility. During times of instability, we are driven to seek balance, which is the vacuum we crave to eliminate our unstable situation and to foster personal growth. Growth does not exist without the vacuum. Without instability the best we can expect out of life is a boring sleigh ride. By embracing the discomfort of the gap between instability and balance we can reach new heights in our lives.

During times of instability we are driven to seek balance, which is the vacuum we crave to eliminate our unstable situation and to foster personal growth.

RISING UP

My good friend, Jan Johnson, recently had her third cancer surgery at the Mayo Clinic in Scottsdale, AZ. She is an amazing friend and business woman, and each time we get together we have insightful conversations about life and business. When I went to visit her in the hospital in Arizona, she said to me,

"The further someone is from what they are meant to be doing, the more challenges they will experience."

Our challenges keep us moving towards what we are meant to be doing by teaching us the lessons necessary to grow. As long as they don't hold us down or stop us, we can use the feedback offered to us through our tough times to find our true gift. The gift of lift.

CHAPTER 5

There Is No Luck!

In late June 2015, I attended the regionals for American Ninja Warrior in Las Vegas at the outdoor MGM Fairgrounds. My friend, Almas Meirmanov, was competing. He also performs as an acrobat in a well-known show at Caesar's Palace. It was a warm, early summer night and the energy of the music and the crowd was electric. The event was being recorded for television and the competition didn't begin until midnight, which was about the time the air started to cool down. The crowd moved in gaggles from one event to the next in hopes to get a view of the Ninja's as they cycled through each obstacle.

Almas had been practicing four hours a day, six days a week for months in preparation for this competition. His wife, Katia, was standing with me along with about fifteen people from the cast of the show he stars in on the Vegas strip. The strongman was there. He was ripped. The young bubble girl from England was wearing a crop top and black jeans that hung low on her hips. She had a nose piercing and smiled a lot. And Almas's Aerialist team was there of course. Fat Frank and Andrew came to support their partner from their high wire act.

Almas had successfully completed the first two obstacles and the crowd was silent in anticipation as he entered into the third obstacle called the Spider Wall. A significant amount of dust had kicked up from the moving crowd. Bright lights mixed with dust at a fairground always adds to the effect.

Almas is an accomplished acrobat and gymnast. He has been training all his life and also performs two shows per night in the big tent at Caesar's Palace. He comes from a bloodline of circus performers from Russia. His father was a circus performer. His sister also competes at a high level. His wife is a contortionist from Russia as well. These are high level and very disciplined athletes. They train incessantly and leave nothing to chance.

As Almas entered the third obstacle, silence fell over the crowd. My muscles tensed and I held my breath as Almas made the leap. And fell. In a quarter of a second it was over.

NOT HIS LUCKY NIGHT?

Katia flung her hands in the air and grimmaced while grabbing her hair. After gaining her composure we began to walk over to where we could meet Almas and offer some condolences. She moved quickly through the crowd. I had to run to keep up with her! Without even thinking I said to her, "I guess this wasn't Almas's lucky night."

And then I got the look.

THERE IS NO LUCK

For years I always believed there was an element of luck in everything we do. But I had never gotten the perspective of an accomplished contortionist or acrobat from Russia! Without hesitation, she said to me, "There is no luck!" In that fraction of a second, Katia challenged my long-held belief and I saw something I had never seen before. It occurred to me that Almas risks his life six days a week in front of crowds of hundreds in his show. He has no room for error. He works without a net. He stands on a chair balancing many feet above the crowd. The chair is on a bar placed on two guys that are on a wire. Luck has nothing to do with his success completing this stunt night after night and week after week. He can't depend on luck. His skills need to be 100 percent for ten performances a week. He can't get up on that wire and say, "Man, I hope I'm lucky tonight!" What if one of the other guys is having a night of bad luck? That wouldn't be good either!

My eyes opened up to a whole new point of view. I started looking a little deeper at what it means to say, "You must have been a little lucky." By attributing success in a project, performance, accomplishment, etc. to luck we are giving up the personal responsibility to an invisible force that somehow takes over control of our destiny at pivotal points in our life. If I fail, then I must have been unlucky. Can you see that by attributing our failure to being unlucky, then we are no longer responsible for the outcome?

There is a young couple that lives in the Mandarin Oriental in Las Vegas. He's a professional poker player and she calls herself The Ladies Coach. I found out

Can you see that by attributing our failure to being unlucky, then we are no longer responsible for the outcome?

through the grapevine that they are members of Tony Robbin's Platinum Partners. The Platinum Partners are an elite group of entrepreneurs that have chosen to pay about $60,000 to be included in a group that travels with Tony and receives personal mentorship with him over the course of a year. This is a couple that lives life at a high level of achievement. They look to be in their late 20s or early 30s.

Andrew has made over $3 million playing poker. I was recently reading an article written about him offering his tips in a game that many would attribute to luck. He worked his way up the ranks in poker from a young age, and now plays some of the largest games in the world, both cash games and tournaments. He scored the first major win of his career at the 2013 Aussie Millions where the ante is AU$100,000 Challenge for AU$1,000,000. The second and third largest scores of Andrew's career came in World Poker Tour events. At the 2012 WPT World Championship, Andrew took second place for $822,375.

For this article, Andrew took the time to discuss what makes a great poker player, outlining six key characteristics:

First off, I'd like to say that I don't think I'm a great poker player. I have been outplayed thousands of times, and some of my opponents constantly outplay me. I tilt, play in bad games, gamble too much, drink too much, and make countless other bad decisions, but I am blessed to know some great poker players. Here are traits they all share.

Experience

This is by far the most important attribute in becoming a great poker player. It is impossible to become a great poker player without putting in thousands of hours at the table and seeing millions of hands. Due to the nature of online poker, with the ability to play hundreds of hands an hour, it's possible to get experience faster than ever before. You have to play at least 10,000 hours of poker before you have a shot at becoming a great player. The best way to get started is by downloading an online poker room, and playing small stakes.

Intelligence

At the highest levels, everyone's experience and knowledge of the game will be near equal. Whoever can adjust to an opponent faster and out-guess what adjustments the opponents are making will come out on top. This is sometimes referred to as "leveling."

Desire and Willingness to Learn

No matter how much you play, you will not improve unless you actively think about what your opponents are doing. Beyond this, you also need to seek other poker strategies from players better than you are. This can be done several ways through books, training videos, one-on-one coaching or discussing hands with friends.

Ability to Control Emotions

In poker, it is always important to have a logical, analytical reason for what you are doing. Our emotions are not equipped to deal with probability and randomness, which are two defining elements of poker. The ability to control your emotions in order to make the correct logical play time after time is one of the hardest things to do in poker.

Social and Networking Skills

Having a strong poker network is key to becoming a great poker player, as referenced above in the desire and willingness to learn. It will allow you to get into the best games and allow you to make friends with the strongest players who can help you further improve.

Having a "Sick" Amount of Gamble

To be a truly great player, you have to have a lot of gamble in you. You have to be willing to take on players better than you at stakes higher than you're used to. At some point, it is the only way to improve. But be warned, it's also a good way to go broke.

Did you notice that not once did Andrew mention luck as being a factor in his success? Luck takes the responsibility out of the equation.

As a child, when anything bad would happen in our family, my sister would chalk it up to the Adler Curse. We believed that the Adler Curse was a fact. If anything went wrong in our family it was because of the Adler Curse. My sister would even say that we have a black cloud following us everywhere we go. If someone got ill it was because of the Adler Curse. If one of us got a bad grade or made a silly mistake, just blame it on the Adler Curse.

Now I am able to see that there really was no curse. The Adler Curse was a figment of my sister's imagination and I had adopted it as the truth! It didn't really exist. But in some way it was probably causing bad things to happen to our family. It was great excuse for not being responsible for the outcome of our bad decisions. And it would get us off the hook for not handling things that needed to be better handled. Many years later, I recognized that it was all made up and it didn't really exist. The Adler Curse was an imaginary idea that was keeping me from experiencing life to the fullest.

How many people are waiting around for their declared "luck" to kick in? Using the "I'm just unlucky" card as an opportunity to get out of jail free rather than taking 100 percent responsibility will delay your success. In fact, it won't just delay it … it will stop you from having the life of your dreams.

Almas could die or be seriously injured if he depended on luck to get him through each show. It's absurd to consider luck as a variable in a life or death situation like this one.

Amateurs believe in luck.

Professionals believe in preparation and training. They leave nothing to chance. They practice the skills over and over again until they are automatic. They use coaches and accomplished trainers to make adjustments and get better. Luck is not part of the equation.

CHAPTER 6

Based On True Events

There was a man that lived at the bottom of a very high and steep hill. His home sat adjacent to a crystal clear stream. Each afternoon he would sit under the trees on a handmade wooden bench and drink fresh cool water from the stream while taking in the sounds and scents of the lush forest.

AN UNFULFILLED NEED

One day the man heard that there was a terrible shortage of water in the village at the top of the hill and the people were desperate, due to an extreme draught. The afternoon heat was scorching and lack of water had become a big problem for the villagers.

One morning, as the man was contemplating his day, he realized that he might be able to help the villagers at the top of the hill. He had an oversupply of fresh and clean water being sourced by his beautiful mountain stream. So in a moment of brilliance he decided to open a business running buckets of water up the hill. He was in perfect physical shape and he had access to a very large bucket that would hold a few gallons of water. He didn't have huge financial resources to start his business but he didn't need much more than some physical endurance and a big bucket. He figured he could run three buckets a day up the hill and the villagers would pay him $20 per bucket, so he would make $60.

One beautiful spring morning he started his runs up and down the mountain. It was exhausting work, but he appreciated the extra $60 a day he could bring home to his family. He ran three buckets of water up the hill each day for about three months. Everything was fine until one of his kids got into a fight at school and ended up with a broken arm. Unfortunately, they weren't adequately insured so the man and his wife had to come up with a plan to generate some extra cash.

The villagers had a need for 100 buckets a day and although it would mean making a few sacrifices on the home front, he decided to run a forth bucket at the end of each day up the hill. He started early and worked late every day. His weeks were long and tiring. In the afternoon the summer sun would beat down on him draining his energy. He had a thriving business but was also having a tough time staying on top of his schedule. He was so tired after a few weeks that he could do nothing but rest on the weekends.

One scorching afternoon, he was hauling his fourth bucket for the day and feeling excessively tired and dehydrated. He was sweating and some of the sweat got in his left eye. The heat was more than he could handle and he became dizzy and disoriented. He tripped and fell, spraining his ankle and spilling the fourth bucket of water. The pain was unbearable. He could barely put any pressure on it at all. He hobbled down the hill to his home by the stream feeling drained, discouraged and depressed.

THE WORKAROUND

The man at the bottom of the hill would be unable to work for the next two months due to his injury. As he lay on the couch icing his sprained ankle, he dreamed up an idea that could solve a big problem for his family and for the people in the village. He remembered that they had a need for 100 buckets of water a day. He could only deliver four and it was nearly killing him. He thought to himself, *What if I build a pipeline from the stream to the village. I have plenty of fresh water. They have a need for 100 buckets a day. I could cut the price in half to just $10 a bucket and I could easily deliver what they need.*

As he began to heal, he formulated a plan to build his pipeline. He showed it to a couple of friends that told him that no one has ever done that before. They disparaged his idea and talked about how expensive it would be to build and how much hard work would be required. They told him that it probably couldn't even be done on that steep hill. But he believed in his dream, and once he was feeling better he began to put his plans into action to build the pipeline.

After about six months, his wife became very angry because he was working so hard and bringing in no money. He would come home each evening tired and covered in dirt from working to install the pipeline on the hill. He started to question himself and wondered if he should just quit and go out and get a real job. His friends told him he was crazy and that he would never succeed at this outrageous plan. But each time he was criticized he became more committed to his project. Although his wife fought him and his friends thought he had lost his marbles, he continued to build the pipeline. After a year he was completely broke and tired from working so hard. But the pipeline was finally complete.

Almost one year to the day after starting construction on his pipeline, he opened the main valve and fresh clean water began to flow from the stream to the village. The whole town came out to watch in disbelief and was shocked the pipeline was actually complete and operational. Over 100 gallons a day were delivered to the villagers and they were happy and grateful that this man had followed through on his commitment to complete the project. He was able to charge them $10 a gallon and for seven days a week he would earn $1000 a day. $30,000 a month in income flowed into his bank account and the man and his little family were able to take a long vacation on the beach. They took walks each morning. And every evening they enjoyed seafood dinners and drank wine as they watched the sunset over the ocean.

CHAPTER 7

Residual Income 101

The man that lived at the bottom of the hill learned some valuable lessons on his journey that was initiated by a devastating injury. Falling and spraining his ankle seemed like the end of the world when it happened. However, it turned out to be the best day of his life. He learned that sometimes the greatest setbacks result in the greatest breakthroughs. He also learned that the big money is in the distribution and not the sales.

When he was hauling buckets of water, he had a sales business that owned him. He could never take any time off because his income would stop. He was exhausted at the end of every day from working so hard. The day he was injured, he had a big problem because he was no longer able to work. He was in the business of selling buckets of water to the people in the village. He needed his own hands to make money. After spraining his ankle, his livelihood was taken from him. While recovering on the couch, he decided he would get out of the sales business and get into the business of distribution. Once he figured out that he could build a pipeline that would distribute many more gallons of water than he could ever distribute on his own, he realized he was on to something big. Looking back, he could now see that, although he put in a lot of work for an entire year to build it, after the pipeline was complete, the amount of work he needed to put in was miniscule. He tapped into one of the greatest lessons in business:

The money is in the distribution and not in the sales.

The distribution didn't require daily, ongoing work on his part, so he could discount his product and deliver more of it to the people in need. He didn't need to collect $20 a bucket any longer to make money. He could cut his price in half and still make a great profit. A little of a lot is better than a lot of a little. He took a calculated risk and followed through on his vision to serve those in the village. By doing so, he freed up his time and exponentially improved the quality of his life and the lives of the members of his family.

CHAPTER 8

Do The Impossible

Twenty-five years ago you could buy a coffee on any corner in America. Most convenience stores and gas stations sold coffee at 50 cents a cup, and the market was saturated with establishments selling coffee. Someone can sit in nearly any major airport in the world and have three or four cafes within eyesight that all sell various forms and combinations of coffee, espresso, milk and sugar ranging in price from $4 to $8 per cup. Who would have predicted that one company could transform a market the way that Starbucks did?

Suggesting that a company could introduce a product that was eight to twenty times more expensive in a market that was already saturated is lunacy. Yet Starbucks did it.

During the same time in history, if someone were to suggest to a group of friends, "Let's go grab some sushi," most people in the group would have replied, "Ewwwwww. That's disgusting!" Today, there is a sushi place within a square mile of every corner of almost every city in the world. And if you don't eat sushi, you are the outcast. That's just how it is today. In a market that sushi was considered taboo, almost everyone eats sushi today. It's the norm.

If you have been around for a while, you'll remember what would happen about ten seconds after an airplane took off prior to the mid-80s. The no smoking sign would shut off and the back of the plane would fill with smoke like a building on fire as the smokers sitting together lit their cigarettes at the same time. Over the years the smoking section got smaller and smaller until eventually it was banned all together by the airlines. But before this happened, the idea of banning smoking from all flights was a ridiculous notion. Everyone assumed the smokers would cause a riot, if they were asked to not smoke for more than an hour. Today, it's taboo to even consider smoking on an aircraft.

THINGS CHANGE

Things that we might have considered ridiculous or impossible have become the norm. Examples like the ones above are all around us.

My life began to transform the day I realized that things didn't have to remain the way they had been in the past. I refused to accept the impossibility of my crazy dreams. I could apply the same transformational principles that others had applied to trigger radical shifts in my life as well. Here are a few of the things that I considered to be impossible in my life that today are the norm. This is just the way it is today:

Jordan Adler, Best Selling Author
$100,000 per month + in income
Licensed Helicopter Pilot
World Traveler

Future Astronaut
Multiple Dream Homes
Philanthropist

I choose to suspend my belief of the impossibility of things in most all situations. There are too many examples of things that we doubted that came to fruition.

Impossibility serves no one.

Rather than choosing impossibility, I would like to suggest that you choose possibility. Ask the question, "What if?" instead of declaring, "No way!" By choosing possibility, areas that once represented blind spots will come into view as opportunities. You'll see things you never even noticed before. Resources for accomplishing your dreams will appear before you. You'll experience options and choices like never before.

Ask the question, "What If?' instead of declaring "No way!

At times you'll catch yourself slipping back into your old ways. When this happens, it's up to you to flip things back around. Go back to asking the question, "What if?" And start to look for the once invisible resources that are all around you, just waiting to take you to your perfect life.

CHAPTER 9

"I Book Space!"

*T*hree ... two ... one. A loud, dull metal "clunk" and my entire body lifted off the seat for a few seconds as my shoulders compressed into the harness. For a moment, I was light, then in a half a second my weight increased to 400 pounds as the rocket fired. We shifted backwards and the pressure of my body against my seat was equivalent to 300 pounds of sand being poured on top of me. The muffled rocket engine fired like a blow torch being intermittently turned on and off. I had been told that G-Force at Mach 4 felt like your ribs would break. They were right.

The light of the sun shining through the oval windows was warm on my face but quickly slid downward through the cabin as our trajectory shifted. The rocket fire ceased and instantaneously the silence was deafening. I swear I could hear "space." Within two minutes, the sky went from blue to purple to black. As we began to level off, I gazed out the window and saw something I had never seen before with my own eyes: the blue, gentle curve of the earth from 100 miles away.

It was 6:00 a.m. and I exited the elevator of the Marriott Hotel in Salt Lake City. The Starbucks was inside the hotel and I was the first one at the door prior to their opening. Within the next 30 minutes there would be a line of 50 people waiting to get their morning fix. This was convention week, and people had flown in from all over the world to hear the many exciting announcements and to celebrate the successes of the year.

The hotel was quiet and I heard some footsteps echoing through the atrium of the lobby. I turned to see a woman with short red hair walking toward me. "Hi, are you Jordan Adler?" I nodded and she said, "My name is Caroline Ferguson. I'm from Australia."

I asked Caroline when she arrived in the United States and about her line of work. She replied that she is a travel agent. I spent many years in the travel industry and had watched this profession fizzle out with the accessibility of travel booking websites. Travel agents were becoming obsolete because of the internet. I believed that most people were now booking their own travel and weren't hiring travel agents anymore.

I asked Caroline, "How's it going?" fully expecting her to say, "Not too well."

She responded, "Unbelievable! I just had my best year ever in 21 years." I was floored and asked her what type of travel she specializes in.

"Space," she replied.

"Space?"

"Yes, space!"

POINTING UP

At this point I concluded that Caroline must be booking space in hotel rooms and on cruise ships. She shook her head, pointed to the sky. "I mean space!"

I was now intrigued. She proceeded to tell me that she was a booking agent for one of the first civilian space traveler programs. They plan to begin sending civilians into space by the year 2020 and tickets hold a price tag of $250,000. She had sold four of them.

In the back of my mind, I remembered writing a goal down in a journal about ten years ago. As I wrote, I remember thinking, *This will never happen.* I was 47 years old and had "Space Traveler" written down as one of my goals. I didn't tell Caroline about it at that moment. I wanted to get home and find the journal in which I had written this goal.

After the convention and returning home to the mountains of Arizona, I began rummaging through boxes, looking for my older journals. After skimming through about five of them, there it was number eight on the list: *Space Traveler.*

3 TIMES THE SPEED OF SOUND

About a week later, I had an email from Caroline telling me that the some of the people running the space program would be in Las Vegas in about a month. She asked if I would like to meet with them. I said, "Yes, of course!" trying to contain my excitement in my email response.

Three months after meeting Caroline, I met with Rose Kingscote who works in an office with Richard Branson. She pulled out all the colorful brochures ,showing me the photos of the spaceships, the space center and the team. Rose said that the trip would take me 100 miles above the earth and I would get to experience weightlessness, see the curve of the earth and travel three times the speed of sound.

I had written down this goal at the age of 47, many years before civilian space travel was even being discussed. On my 57th birthday, I wired $250,000 to become one of the first civilians in space.

YOU DON'T NEED TO BELIEVE

You do not need to believe your dreams when you write them down. Sometimes your dreams are so far outside of your belief window, they are difficult to write down.

Do it anyway.

Most of the time they won't happen according to your plans. You must write them down, then have faith that everything will line up as it is supposed to. Let go of the outcome and trust the process. Your dreams will be born at the perfect time. In the beginning, you may not trust that your dreams are even possible. Write them down anyway. Put your dreams into words on paper, then have the faith that forces beyond your understanding or control are working to move you towards them each day.

> Your dreams will be born at the perfect time.

CHAPTER 10

Buddy And Garfunkel

When I was seven years old, the traveling circus came to town. In 1966, I was living at 560 Lakewood Blvd in Park Forest, IL with my parents and two sisters. About a mile down the street from my home in our little suburb of Chicago was a giant tent erected in Central Park. It was down the tree-lined street, past the elementary school and just behind the public tennis courts.

Everyone in the neighborhood went to watch the circus when it came to town. I walked down to the big top with my family on a Friday night in the middle of summer. The inside of the tent smelled of dust, elephant manure and popcorn. The live band played loud circus music and the clowns and animals entertained all of us.

At 10:30 p.m., after the big circus parade with the elephants, clowns and circus performers, my family went home, but my best friend, Buddy Mondlock, told me he wanted to play a song for me on his new guitar. We walked through the sawdust, up to the front of the big top and sat under the tent on the stage. He played a Simon and Garfunkel song called "The Boxer." I was inspired and wanted to learn to play guitar, too. I asked my father if he would buy me a used, cheap guitar to practice on. He asked me to save up for it and he agreed to pay for half. About two months later I had my first guitar.

I would get together with Buddy a few times a week after school and on the weekends to learn and play songs. We would sit around the record player and learn the vocals and instrumentals for each song. Sometimes we would sit for hours. We began to perform together and had fun entertaining at our school and in the neighborhood. It was a great way to get girls to talk to us! We could perform the entire "Simon and Garfunkel's Greatest Hits" album.

In his twenties Buddy moved to Nashville and began to periodically perform at the Bluebird Cafe. Many great talents have been discovered there, including Taylor Swift, Keith Urban, Kenny Chesney and Garth Brooks. One night, Buddy was "discovered" there as well. Over the next few years, he wrote many songs for Garth Brooks and even recorded on some of his records.

Buddy was inspired in his early years by Simon and Garfunkel. After a stellar music career together as one of the most popular recording acts of the 60s, the two men split in 1970. They had created many top hits together, toured the world and sold millions of records. Paul Simon continued his solo career and recorded a number of hit solo albums while Art faded into the New York landscape to write poetry. Each attempt to reconcile ended in another split up.

Unbeknownst to Art, Buddy picked up some of his poetry and began to write music to it. Buddy put one of Art's poems, "A Perfect Moment" to music and mailed it to him. Art listened and loved it! He contacted Buddy and asked if he would do a world tour with him with a full orchestra. My childhood best friend, Buddy Mondlock, got Art Garfunkel out of retirement and back on the road! They recorded an album together, toured the world and Art sang some of Buddy's songs.

Thirty years after sitting around the record player, dreaming that we were Simon and Garfunkel, Buddy was touring with Art in front of crowds of thousands and Art was singing Buddy's music.

Buddy wrote a song called, "The Kid" that Art recorded on one of his albums. "The Kid" has a line in it inspired by the few minutes we sat under the big top in Park Forest, IL.

"I'm the kid who ran away with the circus. Now I'm watering elephants. But I sometimes, lie awake in the sawdust, dreaming I'm in a suit of light. Late at night in the empty big top, I'm all alone on the high-wire. Look he's working without a net this time. He's a real death defier."

Buddy made his dream come true. He had been preparing for years. He mastered the art of song-writing and performing. He recorded many albums. He moved to Nashville where much talent is discovered. He got gigs at the Bluebird. He took Art's poetry and wrote music to it. He mailed it to Art. He took steps to continue to grow as an artist and put himself in situations that could move him closer to his dreams. The seed was planted when Buddy was a child, sitting around a record player. It germinated as he became an accomplished artist. He never neglected it. He continued to work on himself. As he prepared, practiced and performed, not only did he become better; he put himself in a position to meet the people that could help him get closer to his dream. And when everything lined up as it was supposed to, Buddy was able to live out an impossible childhood dream that couldn't possibly have been predicted.

CHAPTER 11

Who's That Guy?

I didn't know a single famous person. Not one. I had never been to Hollywood. I can't act. Yet at the age of 25, I wrote down on my dream list: *"Walk the Red Carpet at the Academy Awards!"*

In other words, I projected into my future the image of *me* walking the gauntlet of photographers in a tux alongside the movie stars. Hahaha. Was this some kind of a joke? I didn't tell a single person about it because it was so outrageous that I knew my friends would laugh at me for even bringing it up. I had no business writing down a dream as outrageous as this one!

Twenty-five years, later I was socializing with some friends after an event in the lounge at Bally's Hotel and Casino in Las Vegas. I was sitting across from a woman who introduced herself as Gwen. The music coming from the casino was loud and it was hard to have a conversation. But as we got to know each other, she told me that she was a voting member of the Academy Awards and a movie producer. I was curious about her background and experience in Hollywood and began to ask her some questions. At some point in our conversation, she casually said, "Maybe someday I will put us in the lottery to go." I left it at that. I experienced a tiny tinge of excitement, knowing that for the first time in my life my dream was possible.

THE LOTTERY

Over the next two years I became close friends with Gwen but the topic of The Oscars was never brought up. She lived in LA and I was living in Phoenix. We would periodically meet for coffee or lunch, when my travels brought me to southern California.

One weeknight about 9:30 p.m., I was cleaning dishes after dinner when the phone rang. It was Gwen. She asked if I liked the idea of her entering us into the lottery for the next Academy Awards. You can guess what my answer was!

A month later, Gwen called to inform me that we did not get picked to attend. I wasn't too disappointed because I really didn't believe that we would be attending.

ONE OF THE MOST EXCITING PHONE CALLS OF MY LIFE

Over a million people want to attend the Oscars each year and only about 2500 are invited. A few hundred get to walk the red carpet.

About four months later on a Friday night, I was in Atlanta with my friends, Kody Bateman and Dave Smith, preparing for a big event on Saturday. The Academy Awards were on Sunday. We were enjoying dinner and at 11 p.m. my cell phone rang. It was Gwen. Before picking up, I turned the phone so that Kody and Dave could see the screen and said to them, "It's Gwen, she's calling to tell me we are going to the Oscars on Sunday!" I picked up and she told me that, although we weren't selected in the lottery, we had been picked as alternates.

TWO SMALL PROBLEMS

I had two minor problems. One, I would be teaching a seminar in Atlanta all day on Saturday, and would need to be in LA on Sunday morning. Two, I didn't bring my tux. I didn't even own a tux. And no one gets in to the Academy Awards without formal attire. So I asked myself two questions: How can I get to Los Angeles by Sunday morning after teaching all day on Saturday in Atlanta? And where am I going to get a tux that fits me within the next 36 hours?

I hung up with Gwen and immediately called American Express Travel. They found me a night flight on Delta that would allow me to fly from Atlanta to LA arriving at 6:30 a.m. Problem one solved.

About two years prior, I remembered being measured for custom clothes by a guy in Las Vegas named Alex. I couldn't remember his last name but suspected he may still be in my phone. I had never ordered any clothes from him.

It was a long shot, but I found Alex in my phone and called. He picked up! I told him I would be putting him to the test. I explained that I needed a tux in my size with all the accessories and shoes in a hotel room in LA on Sunday morning at 10 a.m. He told me it would be a stretch but would try and make it happen.

He and his son worked through the night to make me a tux and then his son drove it from Vegas to LA and had it waiting for me in the closet at the Georgian Hotel in Santa Monica. My flight arrived on schedule and by 1030 a.m. I was getting cleaned up and dressed for the main event. I was picked up in a white stretch limo and we were off to the Oscars!

Upon arrival, the crowds lined the streets and the police barricades were opened to allow us access. Thousands of fans gathered along the route of Bentleys, Rolls Royces, Cadillac stretch limos and Maserati's in hopes of catch a quick photo or autograph. As we turned the corner, two giant Oscars framed the entrance to where the wide red carpet began. Hundreds of paparazzi were lined up on both sides in the stands and the stars were shining brightly!

The moment I had dreamed of all my life was now happening. I stepped out of the limo and put my feet down onto the red carpet.

Security was all around, keeping the fans from getting too close to the celebrities. A wall of photographers produced a firestorm of glittering flashes as news reporters shoved microphones into the path of the most recognizable stars. The red carpet was long and I relished in each step. It led us into a large, beautiful ballroom where a cocktail party ensued prior to the awards ceremony. I shook hands with James Cameron. I spent a few minutes with Wolfgang Puck and got a hug from Sharon Stone.

If we had been picked in the lottery as Gwen had planned, we would have been assigned a normal seat in the audience. But, because we had been picked as an alternate, we were standing in for two very famous people. To this day, I don't know who they were, but I do know they were seated eight rows in front of Donald Trump and I snuck a picture to prove it!

My written goal didn't say, "Attend the Academy Awards" It said, "Walk the red carpet at the Academy Awards!" Being chosen as an alternate, we walked side-by-side on the red carpet with Scarlet Johansson, Russell Brand, Wolfgang Puck, Jesse Eisenberg and Sharon Stone. The stands sparkled as the gauntlet of photographers shot thousands of photos along the star studded carpeted walkway leading up the stairs to an elegant ballroom, where we could mingle and chat with our movie star peers.

I didn't plan for this event. I could not have predicted it. I wrote down this goal many years earlier. Deep in my subconscious mind I was open to it, but couldn't ever have possibly figured out how it would happen. It was unlikely and illogical. But that is usually how your dreams will occur when you commit to them and then just believe that they are possible.

CHAPTER 12

How To Own Beach Homes All Over The World For The Price Of A Down Payment

About 25 years ago before I had ever received a check from Network Marketing, I had an idea that sounded like a good one, once I started making some money. I wanted to start buying beach homes in all parts of the world. My plan was to put them under management as vacation rentals. Then, when I wanted to use one, I would book it and stay whenever I wanted to. For years, I really couldn't do much with this idea other than dream a lot about it. I would look at real estate magazines and paid especially attention to the beach properties. Once I started making a little money I began looking at properties. Each time I found one that was interesting, I would learn that the down payment was in the range of $600,000 to $1 million and getting a loan was beyond my reach. I was in San Diego and had looked at a handful of multi-million dollar beach homes, and the last home was on Mission Beach. It was a three-level, all glass property with an outdoor gas fire pit and a modern curved facade. The balconies faced the boardwalk. After ten years of looking at properties like this one, I was getting frustrated and had made no headway on my dream.

EQUITY ESTATES

The cab dropped me off at the airport and I headed over to the ticket counter to print my ticket. After checking in, and in a moment of let-down, I purchased a magazine called "The Robb Report" just before boarding my flight. It's interesting how a single action like this can radically change the course of your life. "The Rob Report" features high-end real estate, automobiles and watches. While flying back to Phoenix from San Diego, I opened the magazine and began to thumb through the pages. At the top of one of the pages was the heading "Equity Estates." And right below the title were photos of thirty multi-million dollar homes lined up side-by-side, an 800 number and a website. All properties were beach, mountain and city estates. I checked out the website and the next day made a phone call. These guys had done exactly what I had been dreaming about for years, and for the price of a down payment on one home I could own a piece of all of these homes all over the world. It was an equity investment and not a time share.

I met up with their team in Cancun, Mexico, and about a week later paid into the fund, which gave me access to homes worldwide. My investment is a 100 percent tax write-off, because I use it primarily for business. The weekend I wrote this chapter, I was on the beach at one of my Equity Estates properties with my extended family and friends to witness my cousins wedding in Tamarindo, Costa Rica. Casa Cristal is a 7000 square foot glass home with infinity pools. This home is so big and spectacular, it has its own name. It's ½-mile down the beach from the little beach town of Tamarindo. My cousin had no idea I had this home, and when I found out this was the exact town he and Keeley were planning to tie the knot, I offered the home for the wedding party and reception.

We have held retreats, entertained, had awards parties, vacationed and relaxed at these properties. Most of them offer lavish amenities and epic luxurious destinations as part of one investment. One of the great lessons I have learned on my journey is that rarely do dreams happen the exact way that we plan them.

Rarely do dreams happen exactly how we plan them.

CHAPTER 13

The Re-Opening

My dad was a cynic. He despised network marketing. Called it a Pyramid Scheme. As I was growing up, I remember him talking about it from time to time. When I joined my first network marketing company, I didn't know that it was the same thing my father used to refer to negatively. I remember him talking about how important it is to get a good job and go to college. In our family, it was a rite of passage to be college educated . . . one of the most important things in life. So when I found out about residual income and network marketing, it was not too well received in our family!

After joining my 12th network marketing company in 1992, I finally started to have some success. My dad was still pretty cynical and any talk of my business dealings would end up in a blowup. He loved to argue and my career path was perfect fodder for a good argument. My mom would stay out of it.

My dad was turning 78 and I was back in Chicago visiting him in October for his birthday. When I would come to town we would drive in his car to go to a movie or grab some dinner. Well winter was coming and I remember it being unseasonably cold. The Chicago winds were blowing in from the north. The day before his birthday we decided to go out for dinner. We stepped out the front door and walked down to his 1990 Buick. He loved Buicks! His car was getting pretty beat up and when I opened the passenger door it squeaked. I can remember how old the car smelled when I slid into it. The vinyl seats were cold and there was a big crack in the dash from many years of the Chicago weather extremes. As we pulled out of the driveway, the shocks creaked and everything just seemed to rattle on the car. It took a few minutes for the heater to kick in. I looked over and saw that his car had 168,000 miles and he told me the brakes needed to be replaced. Quite honestly, I was concerned for his safety driving in this car.

I had dreamt of a day when I could help my Dad out if he ever needed it. As a teenager, I would borrow money from him all the time. And rarely would I pay it back. So now it was my turn to help.

Upon arriving back to Arizona I visited the Buick Dealership off Camelback Road. A nice salesman named Ken came out to greet me. I told him I wanted to buy a brand new Buick Lucerne for my Dad with all the bells and whistles. I was able to pay cash for the car. I asked them to ship the car to Park Forest, IL and deliver the keys to my father at his home. It made me feel great to be able to do this for my father.

Unfortunately I was speaking at an event in Florida the day my dad's car was delivered on a flatbed to his home. I got a call from him about 10 minutes after he was handed the keys. He was a little choked up and couldn't believe what he had just experienced. His voice cracked a little as he said to me . . . "I wasn't sure if I was supposed to tip the guy, so I gave him $5."

I said, "Dad you just had a new car delivered to your front door and you tipped him $5??" This is just my Dad.

My parents were married on April 29th, 1957 which happened to be my Mom's Birthday. For their honeymoon, they drove a station wagon across the country to stay at the luxurious Valley Ho Resort which was an oasis in the desert off of Indian School Rd. in Scottsdale, Arizona. When celebrities would come to Phoenix or Scottsdale in the 50's this is where they would stay. Rumor had it that Marilyn Monroe and Humphrey Bogart stayed there when they came to Arizona. I was born less than 1 year later. About 2 years after my parents honeymoon the resort was closed down and they put a chain link fence around it. Many years later, I moved to Scottsdale, Arizona not knowing that it was the destination of my parents honeymoon. I knew of the dilapidated "Valley Ho" off Indian School Rd that had a chain link fence around it for 40 years. By this time, it was no longer out in the desert but was surrounded by the modernization of Scottsdale. In 2006 the Valley Ho resort would be re-opening as an original yet modernized restoration destination. And the opening happened to be the month of my parents 50th wedding anniversary.

I called the resort and told them I wanted to book a luxury suite at the hotel on April 29th, 2006 which was the date of their 50th anniversary and the same week of their reopening. I booked the room and then told my parents that I wanted to fly them to Arizona for their 50th Wedding Anniversary and that I have a little surprise for them. I bought their airline tickets and everything was set for their "surprise".

Everything was going perfectly, as planned until I got a phone call from the manager of reservations. Two weeks before my parents arrival, the hotel informed me that my parents would be relocated to another resort that night because Red Bull was booking out the whole hotel for a big party. You can only imagine my reaction to this news! I said to the manager, "You don't understand . . . it's my parents 50th Wedding Anniversary and they stayed at the Valley Ho in 1957 for their Honeymoon. You have to make this happen!" I wouldn't take no for an answer so the reservations manager told me he would have to escalate the situation because as it stands, they will be the only people in the hotel over the age of 30 and its going to be a wild party for three days! He said that no one that was not with Red Bull would be allowed in the resort. So the next day I had a similar conversation with the General Manager of the property. We argued for 30 minutes and just before hanging up he told me he would need to review this with his team and get back to me. On April 28th, the day before my parents anniversary I received a call from the general manager informing me that my parents would be allowed to stay as long as they are aware that there will be a big party going on.

So when they arrived, I told them that the party was in honor of their 50th anniversary and they had a blast. Because they were in their 70's and everyone else was in their 20's and 30's everyone knew why they were there. They were treated like royalty by all the Red Bull employees and the hotel staff. Everything was perfect.

So Beach Money is pretty good, but to be able to do things like this for your parents is Better Than Beach Money.

CHAPTER 14

How Much Is A $100 Bill Worth?

What someone is willing to pay for something always comes down to what value they see in it for themselves. And we all place varying values on different things. The words that are used to describe what we are selling make a difference. For example, if I am selling you flowers and I say, "You can set the flowers on the table in the middle of the room," you may be willing to give me a set amount for them. If I say, "These flowers will bring balance and color to the room and your living environment will come to life," you very likely will pay more for them.

I called my assistant Megan and told her I would be auctioning off a $100 bill for $1,000 on our conference call on Monday night. Her reaction was, "That's kind of a dumb idea! No one will ever pay more than $100 for a $100 bill!"

The night of the auction she was in her home office and I was in mine. The bids would be texted to her from the 200 or so participants that were with us on the call. I started by telling everyone that this is a real auction. In other words, if someone wins the bid, they have to pay real money for the $100 bill. Bids would be texted to Megan and she would announce them as they came in. The starting bid was $50. A few bids came in. Then I raised it to $75. Believe it or not, there were a couple of people that bid $100 for the $100 bill!

At this point, the interest began to wane so I raised the stakes. I told everyone that I would sign the bill. I was then able to increase the bid to $150, then $ 200 and eventually $300. I soon found out what my signature was worth to this group of people!

At this point, I wanted to test the limits so I told the team that I would have the founder of our company and all the top ranked earners sign it. The bids were raised to $600. I offered to have it framed, then informed everyone on the call that the winner could display the bill over their desk. I said that the bill may bring the winner some luck and possibly even offer inspiration to promote quickly through the pay plan! The bids went up to $750, $850 and then eventually I suspended the bidding at $1,000.

The entire auction was complete within ten minutes. The winner of the bid was a newer distributor from Pittsburgh, Linda Thomas. Linda went on to reach one of our highest ranked positions over the next few years.

The purpose of this exercise was to show that what something costs is not what it's worth. Some people could not accept the idea that someone would pay more than $100 for $100 bill, yet by adding some value to it through the use of language, others would gladly pay between $200 and $1000 for it! In real life we all assign a different value to things offered in the marketplace based on our needs and what we personally believe them to be worth based on what we hear and see.

The story doesn't end here. I decided to try this exercise at a live event with about 500 people present. Following the same process, a man from Great Britain agreed to pay $2,500 for the signed and framed $100 bill. After the auction was complete, I announced to the crowd that the $2,500 would be donated to Network Times Magazine to help expand their subscription base.

A year later I conducted the auction again with 1500 present and the winning bid was $7,000. Two people had won the bid at that amount. We split it between the two, had two bills signed and framed and donated the $7,000 to www.kiva.org to help entrepreneurs in developing countries start businesses through a micro-lending process. The winners had no idea the money would be donated as they were participating in the auction and bidding on the $100 bill.

BOOM!

On Oct 17th, 2015 something unimaginable occurred. The Network Marketing Pro Recruiting Mastery Event was being held at the Mirage Hotel and Casino in Las Vegas, NV. Eight thousand people were in the house and another four thousand were watching through live video stream. Eric and Marina Worre, the owners of Network Marketing Pro, were back stage in the green room with some of the production crew and a few of the other speakers. They were watching on monitors.

I had 20 minutes on stage to do the auction, then a short, ten-minute training on the lessons of adding value to a proposition. No one except for Eric and Marina knew what I planned to do on the stage. I predicted that I could get $25,000 for the $100 bill in under ten minutes.

I started the auction by offering the $100 bill for $50. I asked anyone interested in this offer to stand up. What percent of the crowd do you think stood up? I could never understand why everyone didn't stand up!

I give you $100 and you give me $50. That's a good deal! However, I have since learned that everyone has their reasons. Some people don't believe the offer is true. In other words, it sounds too good to be true. Some are too lazy to stand up—just like in real life. And some just don't have $50 in their wallet or purse. These reasons seem to apply as much in the auction as they do in the real word.

When I raised the bid to $75, more people stood up expressing interest in the $100 bill. More people wanted it when I *raised* the price by $25. When I offered the $100 for $100, about 5 percent of the crowd was still standing.

Why do you think someone would be willing to pay $100 for a $100 bill? If you were to ask each one that was willing to make this bid, they would each have their reason such as, "I may get to go on stage and be recognized." Or maybe it was because it was *my* $100 bill!?

With 8000 people, it was difficult for me to see who was bidding up in the higher seats with the bright lights. By the time we were in the range of $20,000 for the $100 bill, I asked all the bidders to come down and stand at the front of the stage. At this point, there were about 20 people that were still bidding, and the crowd was mesmerized and engaged. There was silence followed by a murmur.

I continued to raise the bid and by the time I had told the audience that I would put a frame around the signed

$100 Bill, the bidding had gone up to $90,000. There were still eight people standing at the front of the stage. I stopped the auction and said, "This is a real auction. If you choose to continue to bid, it means you have the money in the bank and you are willing to give it to me in exchange for the $100 bill. In other words, this is not a game." At this point I'm sure there wasn't a person in the crowd that wasn't asking themselves, *What is happening here?* and declaring to themselves, *This is crazy!*

I raised the bid to $150,000 and then $200,000. At $250,000 a few of the bidders dropped out and at $1,000,000 there were still four people remaining in the auction! Two bidders stepped to the front of the stage in a battle to win the bid. At $3.2 million, the runner up dropped out and a gentleman from Atherton, California, won the bid for the $100 bill.

I brought him onto the stage and asked him where he was from and why he bid $3.2 million for the $100 Bill. The entire auction lasted eight minutes. I informed him and the rest of the audience that his winning bid would be donated to the Starkey Hearing Foundation to fit children in developing countries with hearing aids. The crowd roared with accepting appreciation. This generous donation would help thousands of kids around the world. He and his soon to be wife would spend the next year traveling the world helping expand Starkey's mission.

LESSONS LEARNED

The event was so outrageous that no one really remembers the training that I conducted afterwards. There was a vibration in the ballroom throughout the rest of the weekend that was ignited by the auction.

I learned some valuable lessons that day. I learned that you don't know unless you ask. Neither myself nor anyone else could have ever dreamed that a $100 bill would go for $3.2 million. The auction was vision stretching at the highest level. It was beyond the belief of most everyone in attendance. And none of it would have occurred had I not asked.

I learned that the energy of a single event can completely transform a group of thousands of people. The crowd went from moderately engaged to riveted. Everyone in the room was on the edge of their seats as the auction unfolded. The room filled with light as if the hand of God was upon us. We were collectively elevated to a higher state of being in those few minutes.

I believe that when the auction bid hit about $20,000 it was no longer about the $100 bill. Instead, there was value being created. A handful of people were still interested even after the bill had exceeded $100,000. Some were playing to win. Some were playing to compete. Some were playing for the recognition. And some were playing for a higher purpose that transcended "getting" something.

There was no question that the winning bidder saw a higher purpose in this exercise. He knew that something good would be done with his $3.2 million and that lives would be changed forever. The audience and I could feel his generosity in the moment, although no one knew what the money would be used for during the bidding. He also saw value of being "all in" no matter what. He felt there was a personal lesson he had to prove to himself. He has no regrets. Although he gave away more than one half his net worth in eight minutes, his life has already transformed as a result of this event.

CHAPTER 15

Hovering

The idea of flying helicopters sounded really fun. Nothing could have prepared me for my journey. In fact, if someone had told me how hard it was going to be, I probably would have quit before getting started. I needed a new hobby and I was looking for something challenging that would stretch me. I definitely got what I was looking for! I had also publicly declared that I would be getting my helicopter license so I could take my friends up for fun when they came to town. For years I had been preaching, "See the job through!" "Don't quit until it's done!" and "Do what you say you are going to do!" There was no backing out of this After telling the world that I would be getting my helicopter license, I was faced with one hurdle after another that made me want to quit. I can't count the number of times I asked my instructor, "Am I really going to be able to do this?"

On my third day of training, my 23-year-old flight instructor, Travis Van den Broeke, told me that I would be learning to hover. Looks simple enough: Lift the helicopter up off the ground and hold everything steady.

The "collective" controls the pitch of the helicopter blades that dictates whether the helicopter lifts up or goes down. Pull up on the collective and the helicopter wants to go up. Lower it down and the helicopter wants to go down. The "cyclic" controls the tilt of the main rotor. When the cyclic is pushed forward, the main rotor tips forward and the helicopter wants to go forward. When the cyclic is pulled back, the main rotor tips to the rear and the helicopter wants to go backwards. The same holds true for making the helicopter go right and left. It is kind of like a joystick.

However, the helicopter is suspended from the main rotor shaft; even the slightest movement moves the helicopter forward, back, left and right. Overcompensating causes the chopper to swing like a pendulum. This swinging has a name: *Porpoising.*

The minor adjustments made to the controls are so small, they are almost undetectable by the naked eye. This requires a keen anticipation of what you expect the helicopter to do. It's easy to over control and cause the helicopter to "swing" out of control. Then there are the foot pedals that control the yaw of the helicopter. Push the right pedal in and the helicopter wants to yaw to the right. Push the left pedal in and the helicopter wants to yaw to the left. Well, our brains are not wired for all of these sensitive movements happening at the same time!

Travis then said to me, "I'm going to handle the collective and the foot pedals. The only thing I want you to do is control the cyclic." This meant that I would be controlling whether the helicopter goes forward, back, left or right. And that was all I would be doing the first time through. He then said, "If you can keep it within a football field I'll buy you a pizza!"

Well that is certainly reassuring! But at the same time, it looked so easy. I said to myself, "*I got this!*

Travis looked at me. "You have the controls."

"I have the controls."

He then repeated, "You have the controls."

Within about one quarter of one second the helicopter swung out of control far to the left. He grabbed the controls and within a fraction of a second, we were hovering motionless.

"Okay, let's try this again . . . you have the controls."

"I have the controls!" I said.

"You have the controls," he repeated.

Once again, within a millisecond the helicopter tipped and went hundreds of feet to the right! At this point, I realize that this is going to be tougher than I thought.

We repeated this drill about fourteen times and I couldn't seem to get it. He gave me all kinds of mind tricks to help me. He told me to pretend I am holding a cup of water and I need to move the cup ever so slightly without creating a ripple in the water. That didn't work too well. He then told me to pretend I was balancing a golf ball on the top of my hand controlling the cyclic stick. I wasn't too good at that one either.

Then it dawned on me: I am just in charge of one part of the helicopter controls. Eventually I'm going to need to control the foot pedals and the collective pitch all simultaneously!

Travis suggested that I not "over control" the helicopter. The movements needed to be so tiny, they were almost like a mere thought. Okay great. Let's try again. Well this went on for about 30 minutes until I was so frustrated and tired that we called it quits.

This is what was going on in my brain on my drive home that day:

What if I'm not capable of this? What if I'm not cut out to be a helicopter pilot after all? I have already told my friends that I'm going to do this? How will it make me look if I quit? Am I being a hypocrite if I quit now? I teach people to never quit on a bad day. I'm not sure I can do this. Hovering is just one skill out of hundreds that I need to master. If I can't do this, how am I ever going to do all the others? Am I too old to master this? What was I thinking? Was this a bad idea? I should have never taken on this challenge. I may be in over my head. Ugh.

The next day, we went at it again and once again, I couldn't get it. The helicopter danced all over the ramp. The goal was to have it stay in one place about four feet off the ground.

After about three hours of hover training, Travis said to me, "I can't teach you how to do it. You just have to do it 'til you get it."

Finally, after about ten hours of attempting to hover, in a moment I was dialed into hovering. My brain rewired itself and I got it!

> "I can't teach you how to do it. You just have to do it til you get it!

Today, it is like an unconscious habit. It requires no thinking and it's actually easy. It's automatic. For many hours I felt like it would be impossible for me to learn. Yet, in a moment, all the synapses connected and I was wired to be able to hover.

That's how it works.

"I can't teach you how to do it. You just have to do it 'til you get it!"

I have noticed that most people spend most of their time preparing to do something. And preparing does little to get you closer to your dreams. As challenging as it sometimes is, you simply have to do it. The only way to grow is to do. Life doesn't happen in a textbook or a classroom. Life happens out in the world.

You've probably experienced or heard that the quickest way to learn a new language is to go to that country and speak the language every day. It accelerates your learning by 1000 percent. The same holds true for anything you want to learn to do. If you have a dream, find someone that is doing it and do it with them. You'll learn as you do. I believe in reading and listening to audios but the fast track is always found in the act of doing.

If you want to build a business, stop thinking about it and get out and do it. You will make mistakes and fail over and over again. It will be frustrating and sometimes feel impossible. But at one point you will get dialed in. Keep going. No one can teach you how to do it . . . you just need to do it 'til you get it.

CHAPTER 16

John Dawson

I was 21 years old and just moved from a small suburb south of the city of Chicago to Phoenix, Arizona. I came with a guitar, a suitcase and $250. I purchased a little Honda Motorcycle for $200, leaving me $50 for food over the next month. I was camping out with an old high school friend at her 400 square foot apartment on University Drive in Tempe, Arizona, until I could find work and a place to stay. I remember stepping off the plane and into the 120 degree Arizona summer heat. I had never been out west, but had heard there was a lot of construction growth going on in Phoenix and felt there might be some good opportunities for work.

One morning over coffee, I was looking over newspaper ads for potential job opportunities and that afternoon I rode my little 200cc two stroke motorcycle across town to the Scottsdale Plaza Resort to learn more about a possible position in catering. Riding a motorcycle in the summer Arizona heat is like having someone put a blowtorch to your face. The air is so dry and hot that within a couple of minutes your eyes become like raisins.

I stepped into the lobby of the posh Scottsdale Plaza Resort and was greeted by a friendly staff member. This was a big step up from the motels that our family used to stay during our annual vacation as I was growing up.

I don't remember the events leading up to this, but at some point on my visit I landed in the luxurious, oak trimmed office of the owner of the resort. He had bookshelves up to the ceiling and a high back, brown leather cushioned chair behind a beautiful oak desk. He had gray hair and a friendly smile. He greeted me and asked me to take a seat in a less impressive chair in front of his large desk.

He asked me a few questions about my family and my background. About ten minutes into our conversation, I began to wonder what inspired this man to become such a successful business owner. He owned one of the premier resort properties in the western United States and also had his hand in other real estate ventures. It was clear by his collection of books displayed on the wall behind him that he loved to read. I asked him to tell me the name of the one book that had the greatest influence on his business life. He swiveled his chair around, grabbed a book from his bookshelf and handed me a copy of Napoleon Hill's *Think and Grow Rich*. After thumbing through it, I attempted to hand it back to him and he put his hand up as if to say, "No it's your's to keep." I thanked him, we finished up our conversation and I left his office. His name was John Dawson.

Over the years, I've read that book four or five times and I still own the original copy he gave me. The pages are yellow from age. It inspired me to go on to achieve a level of success I could have never imagined.

Twenty-eight years later, on a Friday evening in April, I was on a stage, speaking to about 500 people at the Scottsdale Plaza Resort. As I was doing my training, it dawned on me that this was the same resort I had visited in my early 20s and that a guy named John Dawson had changed my life by handing me a book called, *Think and Grow Rich*. I shared the story with my audience. After my talk, a tall, younger woman came over to me and asked if she could have a few minutes with me during lunch the next day. I responded, "Of course." It was common for participants to ask for a few minutes of my time. We concluded our Friday night event, and after pictures and some late night networking we all headed back to our hotel rooms to get some rest so we could start fresh the next day.

Saturday morning came quickly, and by 9 a.m. the training event was in full swing. The room was packed with hundreds of people and before I knew it, it was lunch time.

The young woman came over and re-introduced herself. I expected her to ask me a question or share a success story with me. Instead she said, "Please come with me."

I followed her through the lobby of the hotel and through some glass doors, past a fountain in the courtyard and to the resort pool. At this point she told me she was John Dawson's granddaughter and she had a surprise for me.

As we entered the pool area, sitting under an umbrella right next to the pool sat 80-year-old, John Dawson. I immediately recognized his friendly eyes and inviting smile.

I got a little choked up and sat down next to him. I told John the story of how the little book he handed me had changed my life. Then I thanked him.

From that day forward, each time I read a book that has had a positive impact on me, I give it away. Thanks to John's example, I have given away hundreds of books over the years, and have also purchased multiple copies of some of them so that I always have some to give away.

One of the greatest gifts you can give someone is the gift of personal growth.

One of the greatest gifts you can give someone is the gift of personal growth. Share what inspires you and you will become an inspiration to others.

CHAPTER 17

Around The World By Bike

I met Alistair Humprhies many years ago. He's from the UK, and when he was 24 years old he decided to ride his bicycle around the world (www.alastairhumphreys.com). Alastair rode from England to South Africa, crossed the Atlantic by yacht and then cycled from Patagonia to Alaska, crossing the Pacific by freighter.

Alastair completed his expedition by cycling back to England from eastern Siberia. He traveled through 60 countries, on five continents and covered 46,000 miles in four years! His trip was self-funded and 100 percent of the donations went to "Hope and Homes for Children."

When Alistair was riding through Arizona up from Mexico, the local news station picked up the story that his bicycle was falling apart and he needed a new one to continue his trip. I believe he went through five bicycles on his journey. My good friend, CaSandra Smith, saw the news story and called me. I was inspired and got in touch with Alistair and met with him at the AJ's Grocery and Cafe on Camelback and Central Ave in Phoenix. The special cycle he needed cost $2000 and I decided to buy one for him so he could continue on his journey. We have stayed in touch ever since.

As we sat at the coffee bar at AJ's that morning, Alistair shared with me some details about his journey through the jungles of Africa. He said that there were many times that the ground was so soft that he couldn't ride on it and had to walk for miles in the scalding heat. He talked about being stalked by African Lions. And he shared about times at higher elevations that he could coast down the mountain roads for hours.

Alistair decided he would set such an outrageous goal that even if he fell short, he would have done something substantial with his life. He also didn't know if he could achieve his goal, but he knew he had to try. He started by asking the question, "What if I could take what I love and turn it into a career that would allow me to help people and make money?" His question led him to a life of abundance and prosperity. He also knew he would come up upon obstacles that he couldn't possibly plan or prepare for.

Alistair decided that he would solve them as they came up, and, having never done anything like this before, he succeeded. He couldn't turn around and go home once he started his journey. He burned his bridges and took a risk that was worth his life.

And he won.

What is it that you love that you have been putting off? Have you been waiting for things to be just right before you start?

Don't wait until its too late. This is your life.

This is your life.

Don't wait until it's too late.

What adventures do you want to experience in your lifetime that you have been thinking about or talking about for years but haven't taken action on?

CHAPTER 18

Working Harder Is Not Always The Answer

My home sits on a lush, high desert mountain adjacent to an old ghost town about 30 miles west of Sedona, Arizona. It's a rustic wooden home that hangs out over the cliff with dramatic panoramic views of the red rocks off in the distance. I have large picture windows framing the views, and as the summer sun warms the ground the towering cumulous clouds turn black and torrential rains cool the desert floor each afternoon. Sometimes I open all the doors and windows to allow the warm, humid desert air to flow through my home, bringing with it the fresh scents of nature. Each afternoon the hummingbirds dart from desert flower to hummingbird feeder, leaving behind little more than a blur and a buzz.

"It was 4:15 in the afternoon. I was packing to head out on a trip and the sun was setting over the mountain. The Sedona canyons had turned a bright orange framed by my home's picture windows. I would be going away for about three weeks and I was feeling just a little sad knowing that I would be leaving my perfect high desert "tree house".

Just as I was preparing to close the screen door to the outdoor deck, a tiny colorful hummingbird flew into my living room and buzzed right over to the big picture window. No problem. I'll just shoo him back towards the door.

Thirty minutes later, the little guy was still fluttering around the window. Both of us were getting frustrated. My time was running out, and the hummingbird's days were numbered if I couldn't get him back out into the mountain wild. I went to the kitchen to find a container that would allow me trap and release him. I found a plastic pitcher that would do the trick. Have you ever tried to catch a hummingbird? Impossible! They are way too fast.

Fifteen minutes later, the hummingbird was exhausted and came to rest on the windowsill. I was able to scoop him on to the rim of the pitcher, walk him over to the door and within a few seconds he was free to follow scent of nectar once again.

The outcome of this hummingbird story would be written by the one simple choice he had to make: Fly towards the window or fly towards the open door? One direction leads to enormous struggle and ultimate death. The other direction is effortless and leads to freedom. The hummingbird is an agile little flyer. It knows how to fly with a level of skill known to few creatures on the earth. Flying is not the problem! Yet a simple shift in focus can mean the difference between freedom and death.

> One direction leads to enormous struggle and ultimate death. The other direction is effortless and leads to freedom.

FREEDOM OR DEATH

Our choices can make our journey effortless or they can lead us to experience enormous struggle and our ultimate death. Working harder is not always the answer. In fact the hummingbird that works harder to fly through the plate glass window will perish faster than the one that just rests on the windowsill. Neither option works if the hummingbird seeks freedom.

Yet most people seeking financial freedom seek the answer in the realm of the how-to. How do I learn to fly better? Why can't I fly through this glass? Maybe I need to flap faster or back up and gain some speed. Do you see the problem here? A simple shift in focus can mean the difference between death and freedom.

CHAPTER 19

Invisible And Out Of View

For years, I thought my path to success would be charted by working harder, being better, writing a better resume and getting a better job. I got really good at this game. I could write an amazing resume! I mastered the art of the interview. I did everything possible to please my bosses.

I found out that if I was well liked by my bosses and I did a good job, I would be considered for the next promotion. And I also found out that each time I got a promotion, I was expected to take on more responsibility, work harder and longer hours for not much more money.

This is the career track that most people are on. Write a better resume . . . get a better job . . . work harder . . . do good work . . . stress out . . . die. Just like the little hummingbird that chose the route of the picture window. If I hadn't been there to save it, the humming bird's demise was certain. And in its struggle to survive, it would surely have stressed out and died right there on the windowsill.

Over the course of seventeen years, I would attain small and incremental increases in pay as I landed new jobs and received raises for good performance. I would go from a job paying $15,000 a year to a job paying $20,000. Then a new opportunity would come along and I would land a job paying $28,000. That worked fine until the company that I worked for filed bankruptcy and cut my pay in half to $14,000. I was 34 years old and I realized that most people in their 40s, 50s and 60s were three paychecks away from financial ruin. Like them, I was struggling to pay the bills each month and wondered what would happen if I lost my job. The game of work was not working for me—or for most of the people around me! I was in my 30s and already getting tired. I believed life doesn't need to be this hard.

A TWENTY FIVE CENT BOOK THAT CHANGED MY LIFE

I picked up a little book at a garage sale when I was in my 20s that caused me to begin to consider another option. It represented a different focus, one that could lead to a residual income that would pay me multiple times for working once.

No matter how hard I worked, a job would never lead to financial freedom because a job required me to be there to make money. By simply shifting my focus and choosing to master another type of income, I was able to find financial freedom. I chose to consider a financial vehicle that didn't require my physical work to get paid. No amount of hard work in the wrong vehicle would allow for a lifestyle of freedom. Always remember, you do get what you focus on.

The hummingbird's struggle and death would be directly attributed to the direction of its focus. And the hummingbird's alternative future of effortless flight and freedom was simply a small shift in focus. If you must master something in your lifetime, why not choose to master something that can lead you to financial freedom. By focusing on a vehicle that pays you over and over again for working one time, over a period of years you can accumulate an income stream. In other words, the work you do today pays you long into the future. The work you do tomorrow pays you long into the future. The work you do next week, next month and next year pays you long into the future. With each passing day your income grows.

What would your life be like if you had a stream of income that flowed into your bank account each month? What if the amount flowing into your account equaled your bills? This type of income is not found in the job world. You must be your own boss and you must choose a vehicle that pays residual income. It's the only route to true financial freedom. It's real and it exists all around us. But unless people are open to it they won't see it. Just like the hummingbird couldn't see the wide open door leading to freedom, most people don't see an opportunity that exists all around them. The hummingbird was so focused on getting out through the window, it was blind to the open door that was just ten feet away.

CHAPTER 20

Sailboats Set To Sail

My good friend, Donna Johnson, and her husband, Thomas, own a catamaran in the British Virgin Islands. Having never been there, they had invited me to spend a couple of weeks in the Caribbean Islands on their sailboat. There were five couples. Our captain and his wife prepared exotic tropical meals for us each day and night on the boat. We snorkeled in crystal clear waters and visited multiple islands each day. The sand was powdery white and each island was covered in dense green foliage. Each had its own character based on its size and terrain. Some had very wide and long smooth sand beaches. Others had beaches that were narrow and rocky. Some beaches were large and had steep mountainous terrain, while others were sweeping and charming. Some were tiny and could easily be swept away in a hurricane. Others were only accessible by boat or sea plane.

One evening we had just finished dinner, consisting of glazed island chicken followed by a colorful array of tropical fruits. We were lounging on the boat deck laughing and listening to Bob Marley music. The Caribbean night air felt healthy on my tanned skin. I took a swig of my Red Stripe beer. In casual conversation, I asked our captain how long he had been sailing? He told me that he and his wife had been sailing in the Virgin Islands for 28 years. I began to get curious about the training they had gone through to become sailors. I asked them where they had learned to sail and if they were still in touch with their instructor. Captain Thomas said they had learned to sail in Portland, Maine, and hadn't communicated with their trainer in 26 years. Yet they still continued to sail—with no help from the person that trained them!

INDEPENDENT AND FREE

As the sun set, I gazed out to the horizon and noticed the silhouette of hundreds of sailboats against a seascape of deep orange. It occurred to me that I was viewing just a small visual slice of the sea. There were thousands of sailboats in the British Virgin Islands and millions around the world. As each sailboat set to sea, not even a fraction of them had an instructor present. Yet they all could sail the seas and experience the joys of sailing.

Later on, as we returned to our ocean cabins, I reflected on our conversation. I thought about how many sailors get trained to sail, then never even take their first trip. Some sail for a month and find out it really isn't what they want to do. Some sail for a year, then run out of money. A few run their boats into a coral reef, causing irreparable damage never to sail again. Some sail for five years, then get side-tracked with other hobbies and activities. A handful of sailors decide they love it so much, they want to share the gift of sailing with others and become instructors. About one in a thousand sailors will sail every day for 30 years like our captain and his wife.

Millions of sailors take to the sea, yet few have ongoing communication with their instructors.

AN INSTRUCTOR OF SAILORS

I see myself as an instructor of "sailors." I teach people to "sail" in the "sea" of their choosing, then set them out to sea to experience the freedom of the wind and the waves.

NOT MY JOB

I don't need to check in with those I teach to sail, other than a periodic call for a friendly hello. I don't need to tether them to my boat. If I tether myself to their boat, I will not experience freedom and neither will they! I don't need to bug them if they haven't been out for awhile. My goal is to have people sailing all over the world, and the only way I can do that is to continue to train new sailors month in and month out. I get rewarded as I sit in my boat and sail the seas of the world, noticing the thousands of other sailors that I have trained to do what I do and experience the joys of the freedom of the wind and the open sea.

CHAPTER 21

What Is Better Than Beach Money?

EVERYTHING WILL BE FINE

In the early 90s, before I had signed up my first distributor in a network marketing company, I had purchased and listened to an audio series about network marketing called The Masters. On the front of the album set were the photos of the top networkers featured in the audios. Donna Johnson, Randy Gage, Richard Brooke, Jan Ruhe, Russ DeVann, Tom Shreiter and Sandy Elsberg were some of the top networkers on the planet. For years I admired this group from afar. I had never met any of them. Their training on these audios inspired me to persist despite many obstacles and setbacks. I listened to their training many times over the years. I had a dream to get to know each of them and someday share the stage with them.

NETWORKING, HARD WORK AND GREAT RESULTS PAYS OFF

After years of showing the business, building teams and attending industry events, I am happy to say "The Masters" have become some of my closest friends. We have spoken on the same stages together. We have traveled the world together.

We have shared drinks on the beaches of the British Virgin Islands, and we have cruised, sailed and snorkeled together. I have even flown a helicopter with Richard Brooke! None of this would have happened if we didn't have Beach Money.

But we do have Beach Money, and we don't have to consider the day of the week when we book our travel. We usually don't concern ourselves with how much a trip is going to cost. If we want to go, we go! Our businesses allow us to work from anywhere, and usually we get to stay as long as we choose!

As good as all of this is, when we all get together, we typically don't talk about Beach Money. Beach Money is the vehicle. What we do talk about are the stories and experiences we have created together around the world. We share a common perspective. We live life on a different plane. The miracles that happen almost daily dominate our thoughts and conversations as we continue to reframe the way we view the world. We are in awe of life and our part in it. Often, we are experiencing breakthroughs because we chose to face our fears and release the tethers binding us to our old lives. We chose to look at life from a different and non-conventional perspective—and the stories continue to pour in.

You don't have to change. Things will be just fine. Life will go on. There will probably come a day when you will look back and have regrets. You'll probably wonder if you could have done and experienced more. But those thoughts will be fleeting and then you'll just fade into the sunset.

But I can't say "Nothing lost!" Because there will be a lot lost. You will have compromised on the best part of life. You will have sold yourself short. You will have robbed yourself and those in your life of the gift of your greatest contribution. You will miss out on experiences that were meant for you but got lost in your complacency. Have you ever stopped to think that the most fulfilling experience in your life happened because of a person you met? One new relationship can send your life on a whole new trajectory. Who was it that changed everything for you? A single meeting can set off a chain of events that can rock your world and set you on a whole new course. Your dreams typically will come to life as a result of the people you meet. New experiences emerge through our relationships.

There is a life waiting for you that is just beyond your reach. And you'll never again wonder if you are doing the best you can. You're not. None of us are. A simple shift in focus can change everything in an instant. You'll see things in a whole new light. Opportunities that were once invisible to you will come into view. And as the world unfolds from a whole new perspective, you'll move in a different direction that will lead you to dreams that you once doubted were even possible. If you are the dreamer who is stuck, step back and see things from a new perspective. Imagine looking down on yourself and your circumstances. View your life from a point above. Let go of the past and suspend all beliefs about the way things are and the way they are supposed to be. Stop doubting and start living. Make the shift that changes everything. Your dreams are within your reach. Its really not as tough as it seems.

CPSIA information can be obtained
at www.ICGtesting.com
Printed in the USA
LVHW01s0236090218
565900LV00003B/3/P